THE CHEYENNE PEOPLE

BY SHALINI SAXENA

Gareth Stevens
PUBLISHING

Please visit our website, www.garethstevens.com. For a free color catalog of all our high-quality books, call toll free 1-800-542-2595 or fax 1-877-542-2596.

Library of Congress Cataloging-in-Publication Data

Saxena, Shalini, 1982-
 The Cheyenne people / Shalini Saxena.
     pages cm. — (Native American cultures)
 Includes index.
 ISBN 978-1-4824-1982-5 (pbk.)
 ISBN 978-1-4824-1981-8 (6 pack)
 ISBN 978-1-4824-1983-2 (library binding)
 1. Cheyenne Indians—History—Juvenile literature. I. Title.
 E99.C53S53 2015
 978.004'97353—dc23

                                        2014025646

First Edition

Published in 2015 by
Gareth Stevens Publishing
111 East 14th Street, Suite 349
New York, NY 10003

Designer: Sarah Liddell
Editor: Therese Shea

Photo credits: Cover, p. 1 (main image) © iStockphoto.com/ericfoltz; cover, p. 1 (moccasins) Daderot/ Wikimedia Commons; cover, pp. 1 (pouch), 19 (coup stick), 21 Werner Forman/Contributor/Universal Images Group/Getty Images; cover, p. 1 (dancers) M. Williams Woodbridge/Contributor/National Geographic/Getty Images; cover, p. 1 (turtle) FA2010/Wikimedia Commons; p. 5 Rainer Lesniewski/ Shutterstock.com; pp. 7, 9, 11, 15, 17 photo courtesy of the Library of Congress; p. 8 Barbe-Noir/ Wikimedia Commons; pp. 13, 27 UniversalImagesGroup/Contributor/Universal Images Group/ Getty Images; p. 19 John Hauser/The Bridgeman Art Library/Getty Images; p. 21 Werner Forman/ Contributor/Universal Images Group/Getty Images; p. 23 Buyenlarge/Contributor/Archive Photos/ Getty Images; p. 25 DEA PICTURE LIBRARY/Contributor/De Agostini/Getty Images; p. 29 Mark Wilson/ Staff/Getty Images News/Getty Images.

Printed in the United States of America

CPSIA compliance information: Batch #CW15GS: For further information contact Gareth Stevens, New York, New York at 1-800-542-2595.

CONTENTS

Words in the glossary appear in **bold** type the first time they are used in the text.

ON THE MOVE

The Cheyenne (shy-AN) tribe is one of many Native American tribes of the Great Plains. Before the 1700s, the Cheyenne lived in what is now Minnesota, where they were farmers, hunters, and gatherers. Then, they moved to today's North Dakota, where they traveled from place to place hunting buffalo. The Ojibwe (oh-JIHB-way), a Cheyenne enemy, attacked the Cheyenne there and drove them south and west.

The tribe separated into the Northern and Southern Cheyenne by 1832. Today, most Northern Cheyenne live in Montana, while the Southern Cheyenne live in Oklahoma.

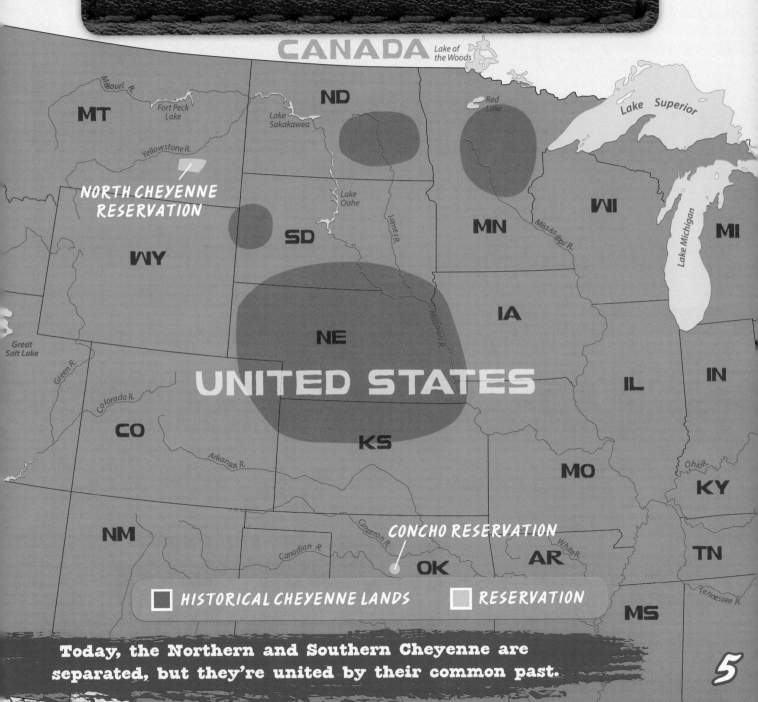

CHEYENNE: A HISTORICAL MAP

CANADA

Lake of the Woods

MT

Missouri R.

Fort Peck Lake

Yellowstone R.

ND

Lake Sakakawea

Red Lake

Lake Superior

NORTH CHEYENNE RESERVATION

Lake Oahe

James R.

MN

Miss&sippi R.

WI

MI

Lake Michigan

SD

WY

Great Salt Lake

Green R.

Colorado R.

NE

Missouri R.

IA

IL

IN

UNITED STATES

CO

KS

MO

Ohio R.

KY

Arkansas R.

NM

Canadian R.

Cimarron R.

CONCHO RESERVATION

OK

White R.

AR

TN

Tennessee R.

MS

⬛ HISTORICAL CHEYENNE LANDS   ⬛ RESERVATION

Today, the Northern and Southern Cheyenne are separated, but they're united by their common past.

5

LODGING

Before the Cheyenne moved to the plains, they were agricultural. They stayed in one place to farm, so they built homes that could last a long time. These were earth lodges, which meant they were partly or wholly covered by earth, or soil.

After the Cheyenne started hunting buffalo, they needed homes they could take with them as they followed buffalo herds. Tepees, or tipis, were the answer. These cone-shaped tents were made of wooden poles and buffalo hide. A village of tepees could be packed up within hours.

DID YOU KNOW?

Europeans brought horses to the New World for the first time.

Usually, Cheyenne women built, set up, and took down their family's tepee. At first, dogs pulled the tepees on sleds called travois (truh-VOY). Later, the Cheyenne used horses instead.

FOOD

As an agricultural people, the Cheyenne grew crops such as corn, squash, and beans. They also fished, hunted small animals like rabbits and skunks, and gathered wild rice, fruits, and roots.

After the Cheyenne began hunting buffalo on the plains, the big animals became their main source of food. The Cheyenne way of hunting changed once they got horses from other tribes. It was much easier to follow the buffalo on horse than on foot. Deer, elk, antelope, and sheep provided other sources of meat.

Buffalo were used for food as well as to make clothing, housing, tools, and more. Here, the Cheyenne honor the buffalo in the Buffalo Dance.

SPEAKING CHEYENNE

The Cheyenne call themselves Tsistsistas (tsehs-TSEHS-tahs), which is thought to mean "the beautiful people." The Cheyenne language is part of the Algonquian family of languages. Even though there are only 14 letters in the Cheyenne alphabet, many English phrases can be expressed with just one word in Cheyenne. For example, "What is your name?" is *netonêševehe* (nih-TOHN-sheh-veh).

All Cheyenne communicated in the same language, and many even spoke a second or third language. Today, few young people speak Cheyenne, so the language is in danger of dying out.

LETTERS OF THE CHEYENNE ALPHABET

LETTER	SOUNDS LIKE
a	a as in "father"
e	i as in "lick"
h	h as in "hay"
k	k as in "skate"
'	stopping sound as in "uh-oh"
m	m as in "mop"
n	n as in "no"
o	o as in "note"
p	p as in "pen"
s	s as in "say"
š	sh as in "shy"
t	t as in "top"
v	v as in "van"
x	ch as in "ache"

The word "Cheyenne" may be taken from a French word that was borrowed from a Sioux (SOO) word.

11

CLOTHING

Cheyenne women wore dresses they made out of the skins of animals the tribe hunted, such as deer, sheep, or antelope. Men wore animal-skin cloths around their waist. Women wore leather boots, while men wore flat leather shoes called moccasins. In winter, the Cheyenne kept warm by adding robes of buffalo skin and leggings.

Beads or porcupine **quills** sometimes decorated clothing. Leaders wore feather headdresses on their head. Cheyenne clothing changed over time. Today, many of these items are only worn during special **ceremonies**.

DID YOU KNOW?

Fringe was added to clothing as decoration, but it also had another purpose. As it moved, it helped keep bugs away!

The detailed work seen on **traditional** Cheyenne clothing
was usually created by women.

13

Games, toys, sports, and education were a part of the traditional Cheyenne childhood. Instead of going to school, children learned from their elders. Both girls and boys were skilled at riding horses from a young age.

Young boys played with bows and arrows. When they were old enough, they learned hunting, fishing, and fighting.

Young girls played with dolls and toy tepees. They learned to cook, make clothes, and do other chores. Girls sometimes grew up to be warriors and hunters like boys did.

DID YOU KNOW?

Lacrosse was one of the most popular games among the Cheyenne.

Toys were used to prepare Cheyenne girls and boys for the tasks they would handle when they became adults. Here, Cheyenne girls are pictured with toy tepees.

15

ORGANIZATION

The major groups that led the Cheyenne were the **Council** of Forty-Four and seven military societies. Forty-four chiefs sat on the council and made decisions to keep peace among the ten main Cheyenne bands. The seven military societies made choices about warfare. The most famous and powerful of these was the Dog Soldier Society.

Cheyenne women belonged to female societies, such as the Quillers' Society in which they decorated important clothing. Other societies focused on other areas of Cheyenne traditional life, such as dance.

DID YOU KNOW?

The Contrary Society was made up of Cheyenne who did many things backward—like saying "yes" when they meant "no"!

Cheyenne warriors had to guard their tribe against enemy tribes and white settlers.

LIFE ON THE PLAINS

Living on the Great Plains meant that the Cheyenne came across other Plains tribes. Sometimes this contact was friendly. The Cheyenne traded buffalo hides for things they needed from other tribes, such as corn. The Cheyenne were also a key part of the horse trade, helping other tribes get horses.

Other times, tribes would fight. This didn't always mean hurting or killing each other, though. Tribes sometimes stole horses or guns from each other. The Cheyenne also had a **custom** called counting coup (KOO), which meant touching an enemy in battle without hurting them.

18

Some Cheyenne used coup sticks like this in battle to touch, but not harm, their enemies. This custom was meant to prove bravery.

CRAFTS AND ENTERTAINMENT

Although the Cheyenne worked hard, they also set aside time for different activities. Making crafts with beads and porcupine quills was popular, and so was pipe-carving.

The tribe gathered to hear stories about the past. Storytelling was a way to entertain as well as remember important people and events.

Song and dance also helped bring the Cheyenne together. There were many songs about **religion**, nature, love, children, healing, and war.

DID YOU KNOW?

The Cheyenne were said to have learned "wolf songs" by listening to wolves. Cheyenne men often sang wolf songs when they were traveling.

Decorating clothing with porcupine quills, or quilling, took a lot of skill and practice.

The Cheyenne religious tradition included many spirits, but the most important **deities** were the Wise One Above and a god who lived under the ground. Many religious ceremonies and special objects reflected their beliefs.

The most valuable items were four Sacred Arrows and a hat made of buffalo skin called the Sacred Medicine Hat. Every year, the Cheyenne took part in two of their most important ceremonies: the Renewal of the Sacred Arrows and the Sun Dance. Some Cheyenne still carry on these ceremonies.

DID YOU KNOW?

The Sacred Arrows were said to be found by a Cheyenne prophet named Sweet Medicine. The feathers of the arrows are replaced each year during the Renewal of the Sacred Arrows ceremony.

Those who take part in the Sun Dance may wear special clothing, paint their body, and spend several days praying and dancing, going without food or water for long periods of time.

When the Cheyenne came into contact with white settlers, their lives changed quickly. Fighting between the Cheyenne and the US military began in the 1850s.

The Southern Cheyenne tried to make peace with the US government. However, many Cheyenne were killed in surprise attacks, including the Sand Creek **Massacre** of 1864. The Northern Cheyenne helped defeat Lieutenant Colonel George Armstrong Custer and his troops in the Battle of the Little Bighorn. However, by the late 1870s, the Northern and Southern Cheyenne were forced to live on **reservations**.

DID YOU KNOW?

Black Kettle was a Southern Cheyenne chief who tried to make peace before the Sand Creek Massacre. He later moved to a village on the Washita River where he was killed by Custer's soldiers.

The Northern Cheyenne and Lakota Sioux fought together in the Battle of the Little Bighorn to guard their lands.

25

Reservation life wasn't easy for the Cheyenne. They were forced to give up their customs. For many years, Cheyenne children were sent to schools where they could only speak English and had to dress like white children.

The Southern Cheyenne went to an Oklahoma reservation, which they shared with the Arapaho. The Northern Cheyenne went to the same reservation at first. Many left to return north, though. Some were killed on the way. However, US president Chester A. Arthur created a reservation for the remaining Northern Cheyenne in Montana in 1884.

DID YOU KNOW?

Although they're separated by distance, the Northern and Southern Cheyenne are still in contact. The Northern Cheyenne guard the Sacred Medicine Hat, and the Southern Cheyenne guard the Sacred Arrows.

Among other problems on early Native American reservations, sickness was common and often deadly.

MODERN CHEYENNE

In the 1960s and 1970s, the Cheyenne finally got more freedom from the US government to make decisions about their future. Many Cheyenne still live on or near their reservations. There are schools for children to attend and businesses to provide jobs. Both reservations depend on ranching and farming for money.

Today's Cheyenne have the same kinds of dress, jobs, and homes as other Americans. However, they take the time to come together to remember and honor the special history and customs they share.

DID YOU KNOW?

The Cheyenne still have to fight to protect their land and resources from outside businesses.

Ben Nighthorse Campbell, a Northern Cheyenne, was a US Senator. He worked to solve issues important to his state and his Native American community.

GLOSSARY

ceremony: an event to honor or celebrate something

council: a group that makes decisions for a larger group

custom: something that people do in a particular way

deity: a god, goddess, or other heavenly being

fringe: a border of short strands or threads hanging loosely next to each other

lacrosse: a sport begun by Native Americans in which two teams use sticks with a net pouch at one end to throw and catch a rubber ball

massacre: the killing of a large number of people, especially when they cannot defend themselves

prophet: someone believed to pass on the will of a god

quill: a sharp hollow spine on the body of a porcupine

religion: a belief in and way of honoring a god or gods

reservation: land set aside by the US government for Native Americans

traditional: having to do with long-practiced customs

FOR MORE INFORMATION

BOOKS

Costain, Meredith. *Native Americans of the Great Plains.* New York, NY: PowerKids Press, 2013.

Cunningham, Kevin, and Peter Benoit. *The Cheyenne.* New York, NY: Children's Press, 2011.

De Capua, Sarah. *The Cheyenne.* New York, NY: Marshall Cavendish Benchmark, 2007.

WEBSITES

Cheyenne Legends, Myths, and Stories
native-languages.org/cheyenne-legends.htm
Learn about Cheyenne myths through this website.

Native American Facts for Kids: Cheyenne Indians
bigorrin.org/cheyenne_kids.htm
Learn the answers to popular questions about the Cheyenne people.

INDEX